ULD WALK TO

TING COFFEE STORE TO

WAS FRESHLY ROASTED

L WARM. COFFEE WAS MY

: I WAS VERY CAREFUL

BEANS INTO GLASS... AND

BATCHES IN MY GRINDER.

LAURIE COLWIN, *HOME COOKING*

ON SATURDAY MORNINGS I

CUP OR PORTO RICO IMP

GET MY COFFEE. OFTEN

AND THE BEANS WERE ST

NECTAR AND MY AMBROS

ABOUT IT. I DECANTED M

I GROUND THEM IN LITTL

"Excuse Me?!" Amani bellowed, "You're blaming me for what happened to my brother?." The older man flinched and looked around, visably uncomfortable. "M-miss," he whimpered, "could you please keep your voice down? You're being disruptive-" Amani flushed an angry purple and before she could think of a retort a loud, soft voice pushed its way through the crowd. "What seems to be the problem here, friends?." "A large women emerged, smiling maternaly. Amani noticed that she had eight thick red tentacles in the place of a tail. "No, ma'am." Amani said coldly. "I'll be leaving now, anyway. I should have known that asking a bunch of lightweight coral-reef idiots ~~prama~~ for help was a ~~trash~~ terrible idea." Amani cut through the crowd, noticing that the women with the tentacles was closely watching her leave.

 CollinsPublishersSanFrancisco
A Division of HarperCollins*Publishers*
From the book *Espresso: Culture & Cuisine* (Chronicle Books)
Photographs by Karl Petzke
Art direction and styling by Sara Slavin
Photograph © 1994 Karl Petzke
Cover excerpt from Ernest Hemingway, *A Moveable Feast*
Design: Barbara Vick Design
ISBN 0-00-225190-6
Printed in China

T NOTHING SUBSISTS,...STILL,

E VITALITY, MORE UNSUBSTANTIAL,

THE SMELL AND TASTE OF THINGS

E SOULS, READY TO REMIND US,

NT, AMID THE RUINS OF ALL THE

HE TINY AND ALMOST IMPALPABLE

T STRUCTURE OF RECOLLECTION.

MARCEL PROUST, *SWANN'S WAY*

...WHEN FROM A LONG-DISTANT

ALONE, MORE FRAGILE, BUT WITH

MORE PERSISTENT, MORE FAITHFU

REMAIN POISED A LONG TIME,

WAITING AND HOPING FOR THEIR

REST; AND BEAR UNFALTERING, I

DROP OF THEIR ESSENCE, THE